POPULAR SONGS

HAL LEONARD
STUDENT PIANO LIBRARY

Country Favorites

Arranged by Mona Rejino

T0081995

ISBN 978-1-4584-0539-5

HAL•LEONARD®
CORPORATION
7777 W. BLUEMOUND RD. P.O. BOX 13819 MILWAUKEE, WI 53213

Visit Hal Leonard Online at
www.halleonard.com

CONTENTS

Always On My Mind

Words and Music by Wayne Thompson,
Mark James and Johnny Christopher
Arranged by Mona Rejino

Slow and steady (♩ = 69)

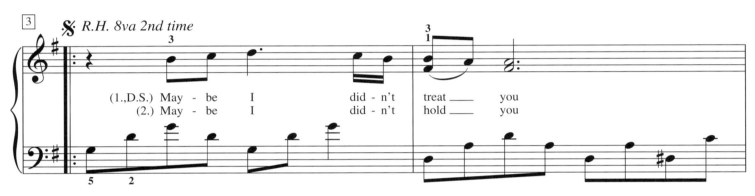

(1.,D.S.) May - be I did - n't treat ____ you
(2.) May - be I did - n't hold ____ you

quite as good ____ as I should have,
all those lone - ly, lone - ly times, ____

may - be I did-n't
and I guess I nev - er

love ____ you   quite as of - ten   as I   should have.
told ____ you   I'm so hap - py   that you're   mine. ____

Lit - tle things I should have said and done, ___
If I made you should have feel ___ sec - ond best, ___

I just nev - er took the time. _____
I'm so sor - ry, I was blind. _____

You were al - ways on my mind;
cresc.
mf

To Coda ⊕ 1.
you were al - ways on my _ mind.
mp
2.
mind.
mp

5

Tell me, tell me that your sweet love has-n't

died. ___ Give me, give me

one more chance to keep you sat - is - fied, _____ sat - is - fied. ___

D.S. al Coda

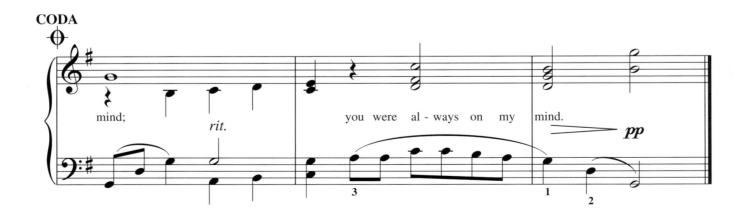

CODA

mind; *rit.* you were al - ways on my mind.

Hey, Good Lookin'

Words and Music by
Hank Williams
Arranged by Mona Rejino

don't _____ you think may - be
know _____ I've been took - en.

we could find us a
How's a - bout keep - in'

brand - new rec - i - pe? _____
stead - y com - pa - ny? _____

I got a
I'm gon - na

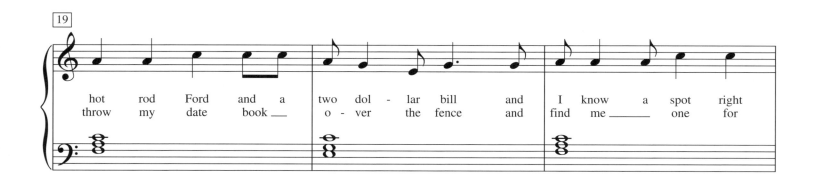

hot rod Ford and a two dol - lar bill and I know a spot right
throw my date book _____ o - ver the fence and find me _____ one for

o - ver the hill. _____ There's so - da pop and the danc - in's free, so if you
five or ten cents. _____ I'll keep it 'til it's _____ cov - ered with age _____ 'cause I'm

wan - na have fun, come a - long with me. ——
writ - in' your name down on ev - 'ry page. ——

Hey, good

look - in', what - cha got cook - in'?

1.

How's a - bout cook - in' some - thin' up —— with me?

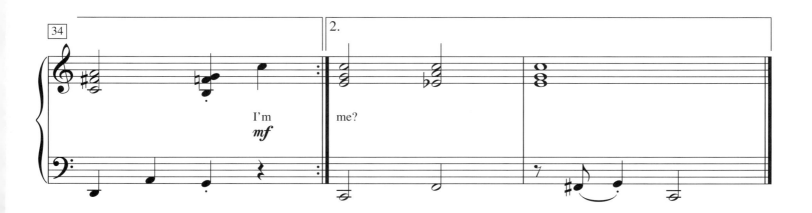

2.

I'm me?

9

Crazy

Words and Music by
Willie Nelson
Arranged by Mona Rejino

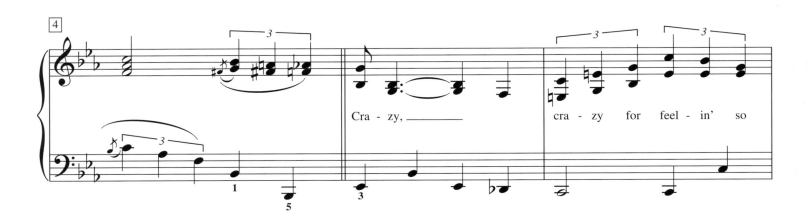

10

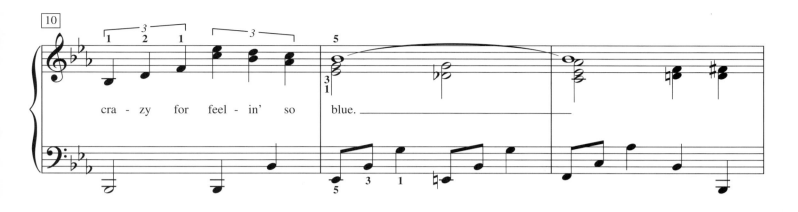

cra - zy   for   feel - in'   so   blue.

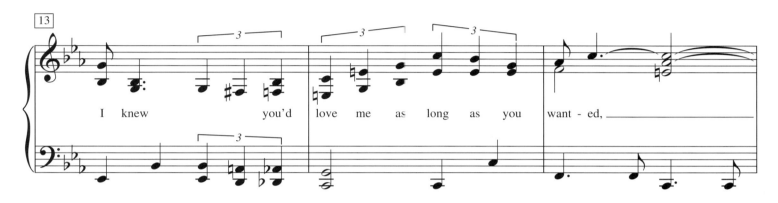

I   knew   you'd   love   me   as   long   as   you   want - ed,

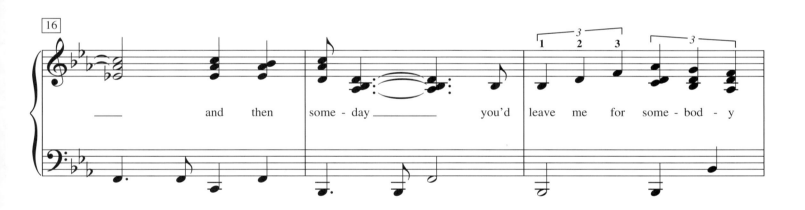

and   then   some - day   you'd   leave   me   for   some - bod - y

new.   Wor - ry,

why do I let my-self wor - ry, _____

won - d'rin _____ what in the world did I do?

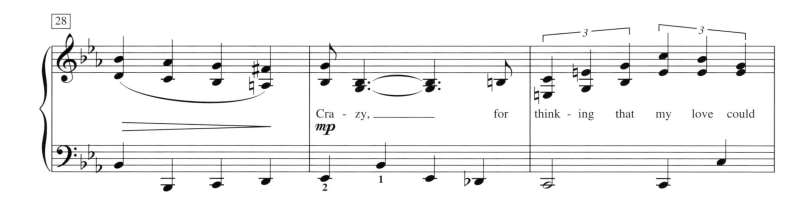

Cra - zy, _____ for think - ing that my love could

mp

hold you. _____ I'm cra - zy for try - in',

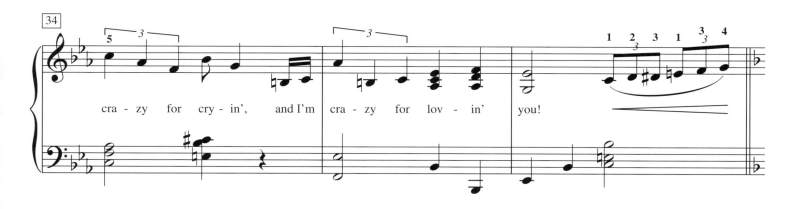

cra - zy for cry - in', and I'm cra - zy for lov - in' you!

Cra - zy, _____ for think - ing that my love could hold you. _____

mf

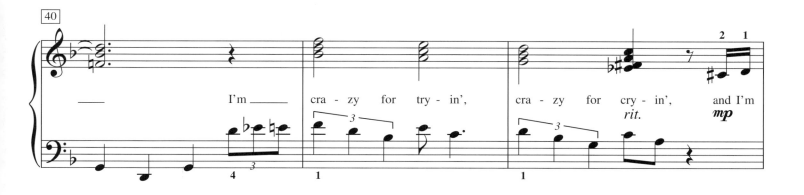

_____ I'm _____ cra - zy for try - in', cra - zy for cry - in', and I'm

rit.   mp

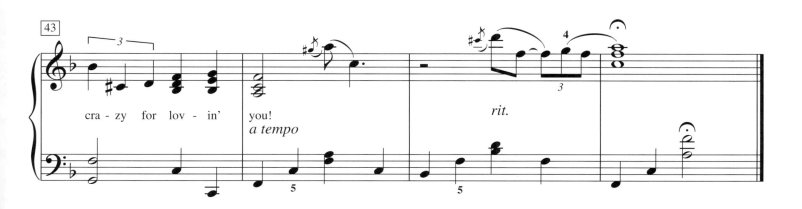

cra - zy for lov - in' you!

a tempo   rit.

Grandpa

(Tell Me 'Bout the Good Old Days)

Words and Music by
Jamie O'Hara
Arranged by Mona Rejino

Moderately slow Country (♩ = 100)

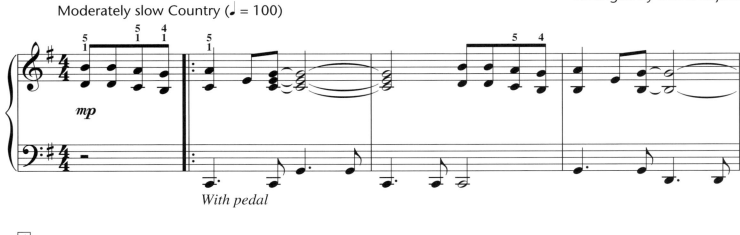

With pedal

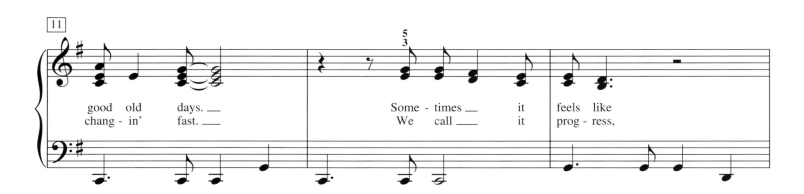

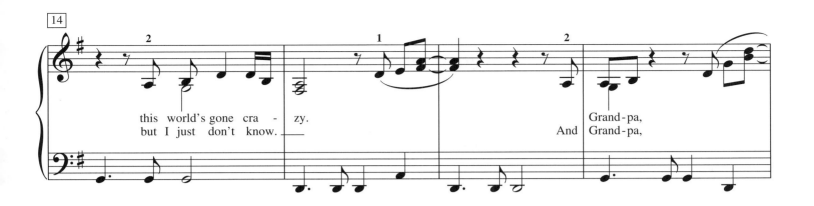

this world's gone cra - zy.
but I just don't know. ___

And Grand - pa,
Grand - pa,

take me back to yes - ter - day, ___
let's wan - der back in - to the past, ___

when the line ___ be - tween
then paint me the

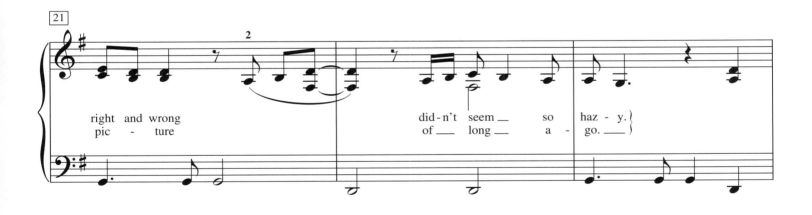

right and wrong
pic - ture

did - n't seem ___ so haz - y.
of ___ long ___ a - go. ___

Did lov - ers real - ly fall in love to stay ___ and stand be - side each oth - er come what may? ___

mf

Was a prom-ise real-ly some - thing peo-ple ___ kept, ___ not just some-thing they would

say ___ and then for - get? ___ Did fam-'lies real-ly bow their heads to pray? _

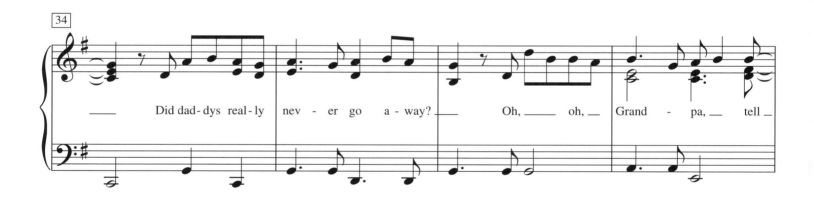

___ Did dad-dys real-ly nev - er go a - way? Oh, ___ oh, ___ Grand - pa, ___ tell _

___ me 'bout the good old ___ days. ___

1.

mp

Oh, _____ oh, ___ Grand - pa, ___ tell _

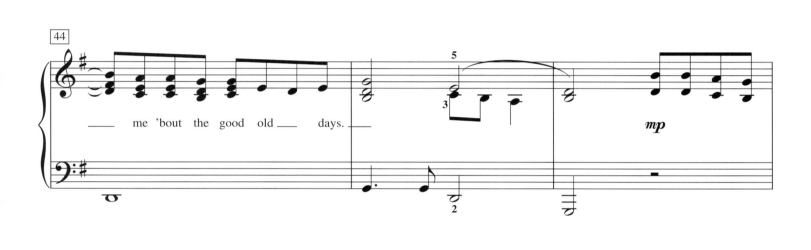

___ me 'bout the good old ___ days. ___

mp

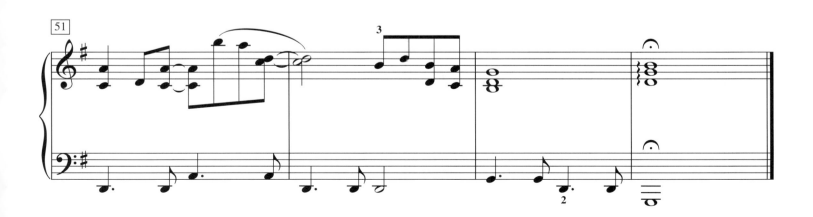

17

God Bless the U.S.A.

Words and Music by
Lee Greenwood
Arranged by Mona Rejino

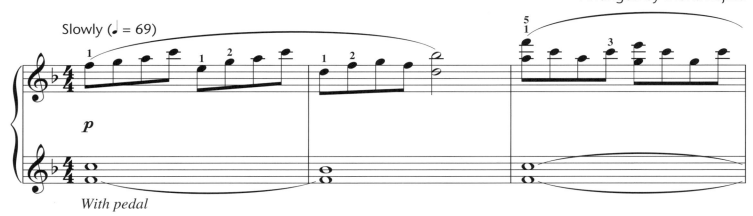

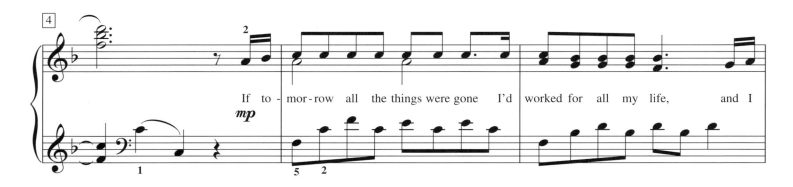

If to - mor - row all the things were gone I'd worked for all my life, and I

had to start a - gain _____ with just my chil - dren and my wife. I'd

thank my luck - y stars to be liv - in' here to - day, 'cause the flag still stands for free - dom and they

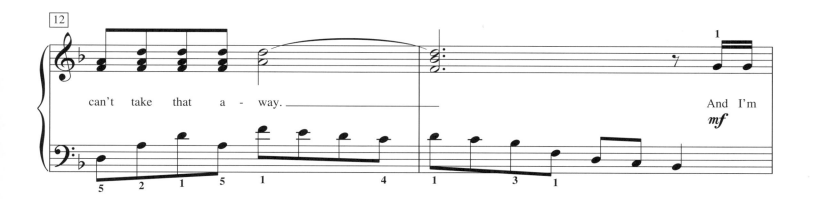

can't take that a - way. _____ And I'm *mf*

proud to be an A - mer - i - can ___ where at least I know I'm free. And I

won't for - get the men who died, who gave that right to me. And I'd glad - ly

To Coda ⊕

stand up next to you and de - fend her still to day. 'Cause there ain't no doubt I love this land ___

God bless the U. S. A.

mp

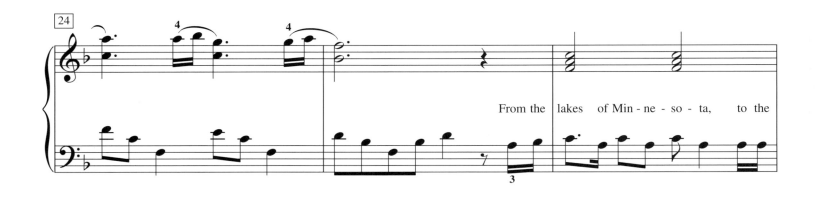

From the lakes of Min - ne - so - ta, to the

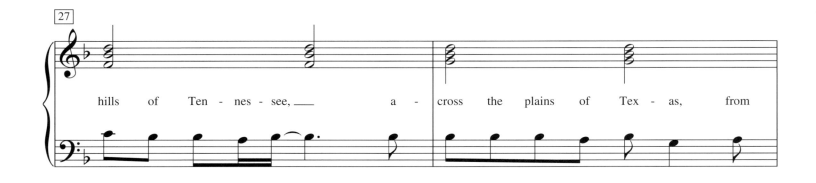

hills of Ten - nes - see, __ a - cross the plains of Tex - as, from

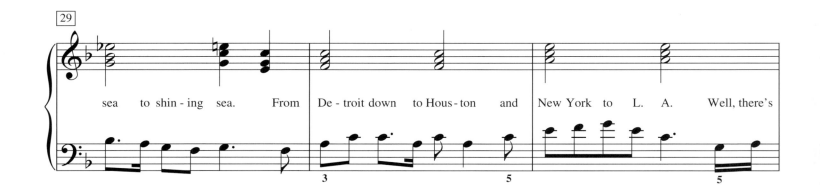

sea to shin - ing sea. From De - troit down to Hous - ton and New York to L. A. Well, there's

pride   in   ev - 'ry   A - mer - i - can   heart,   and   it's   time   to   stand   and   say

D.S. al Coda

CODA

That I'm
mf

God   bless   the   U.   S.

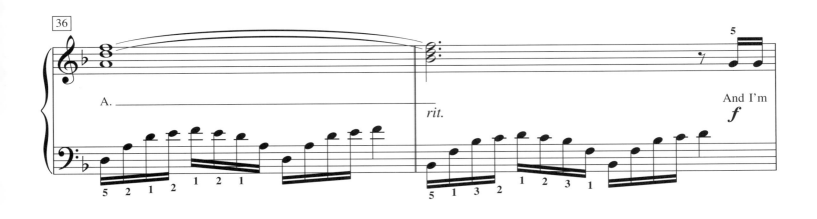

A. _____

rit.

And I'm
f

Majestically (♩ = 63)

proud   to   be   an   A - mer - i - can ___   where   at   least   I   know   I'm   free,   and   I

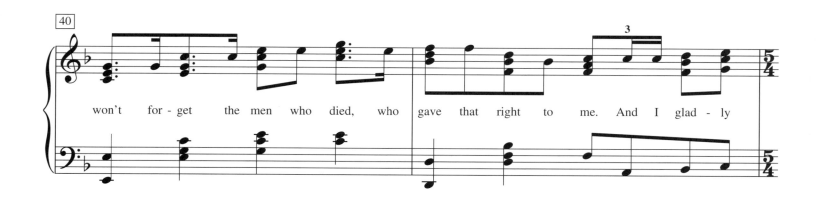

won't for-get the men who died, who gave that right to me. And I glad-ly

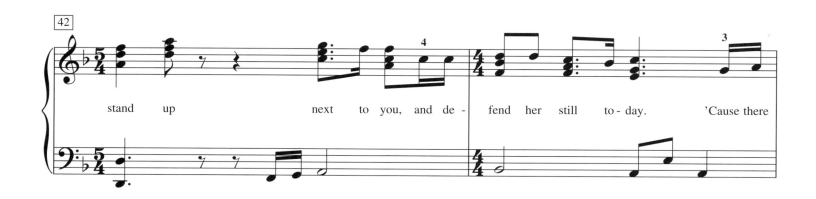

stand up next to you, and de - fend her still to-day. 'Cause there

ain't no doubt I love this land. _____ God bless the

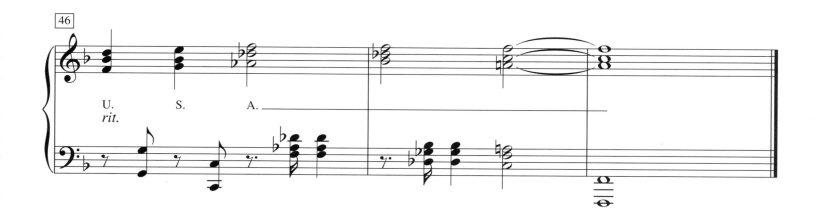

U. S. A. _____
rit.

I Will Always Love You

Words and Music by
Dolly Parton
Arranged by Mona Rejino

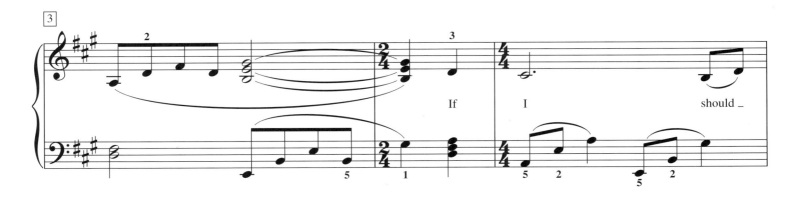

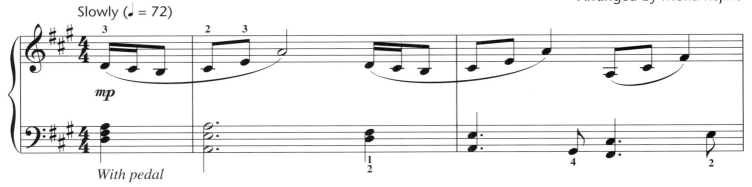

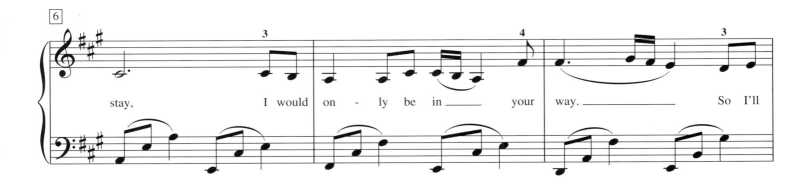

way. _____ And I _____ will al - ways _ love _

you. _____ I _____ will al - ways _ love _ you.

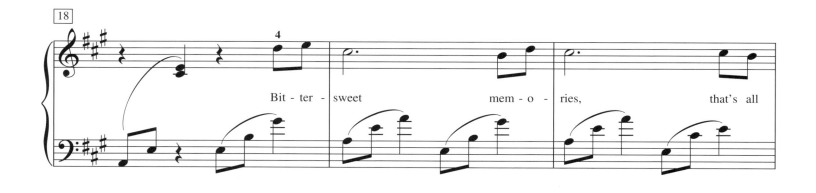

Bit - ter - sweet mem - o - ries, that's all

I am tak - ing with me. _____ Good - bye, please don't

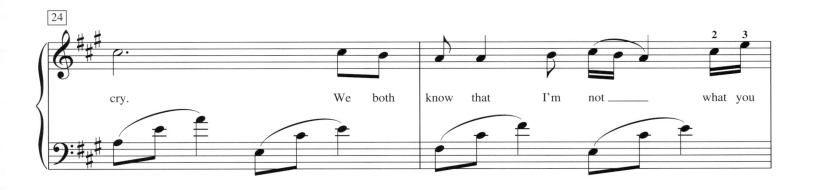

It Was Almost Like a Song

Lyric by Hal David
Music by Archie Jordan
Arranged by Mona Rejino

song.　　　　　　　　You were in my arms,　　　　just where you be-

long,　　　　　we were so in love.　　　　It was al-most like a

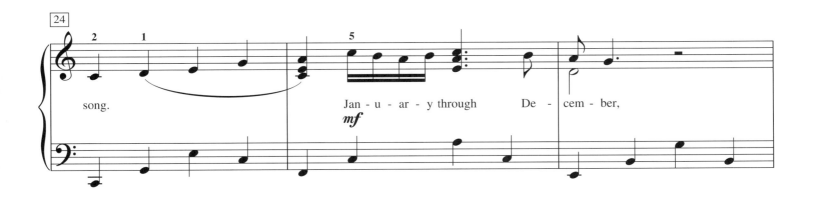

song.　　　　　Jan-u-ar-y through　　De-cem-ber,

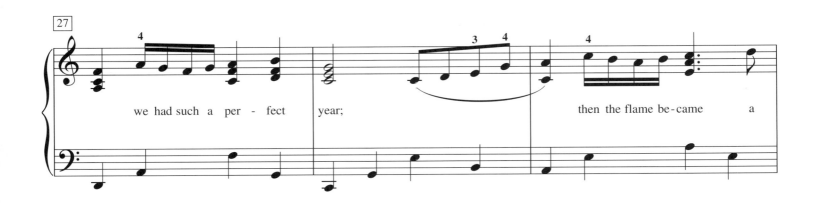

we had such a per-fect year;　　　　then the flame be-came　　a

dy - ing em - ber; all at once you weren't there.

mp

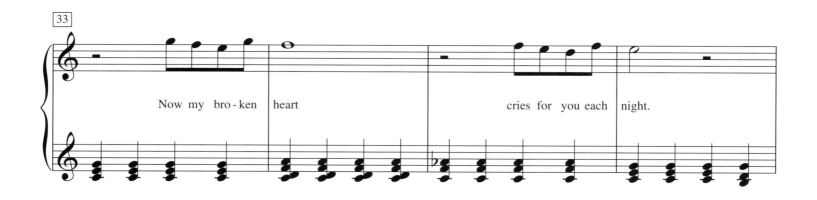

Now my bro - ken heart cries for you each night.

It's al - most like a song, _____ but it's too sad to

write. Now my bro - ken heart

f

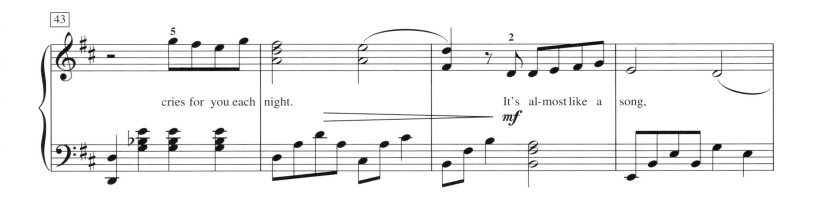

cries for you each night. It's al-most like a song,

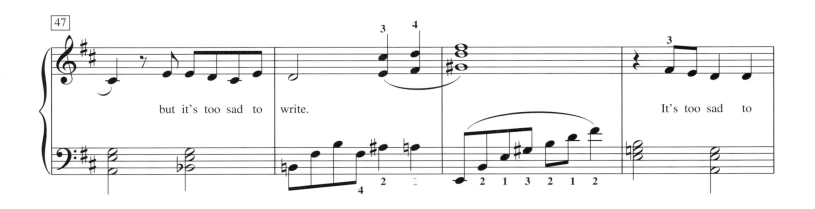

but it's too sad to write. It's too sad to

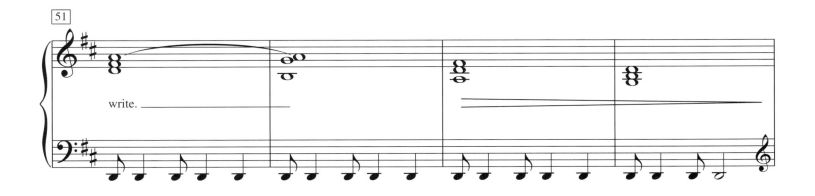

write.

Mammas Don't Let Your Babies Grow Up to Be Cowboys

Words and Music by Ed Bruce
and Patsy Bruce
Arranged by Mona Rejino

Moderate Country Waltz (♩. = 60)

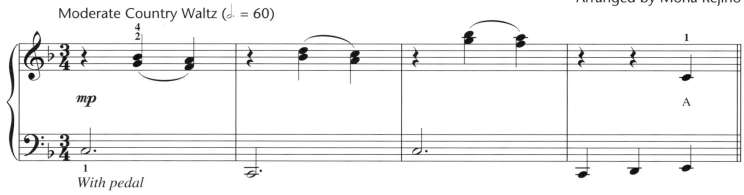

cow - boy ain't eas - y to love and he's hard - er to hold,

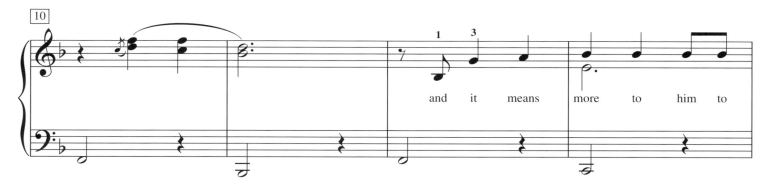

and it means more to him to

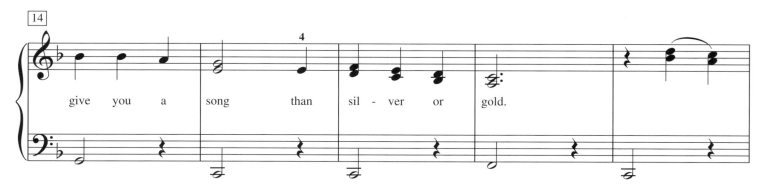

give you a song than sil - ver or gold.

Bud - weis - er buck - les and soft fad - ed

Le - vi's and each night be - gins a new day. If you

can't un - der - stand him and he don't die young, he'll

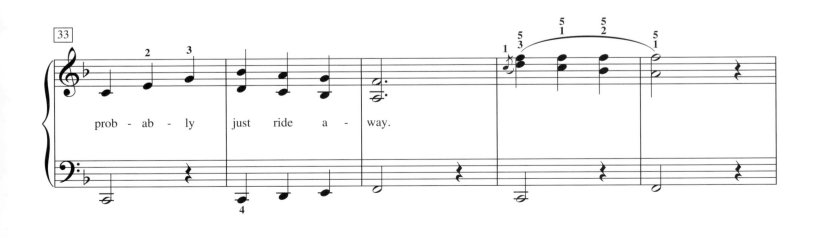

prob - ab - ly just ride a - way.

Mam - mas don't let your ba - bies grow up to be

mf

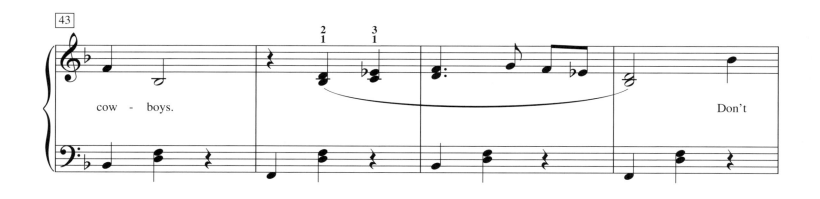

cow - boys. Don't

let 'em pick gui - tars and drive them old trucks.

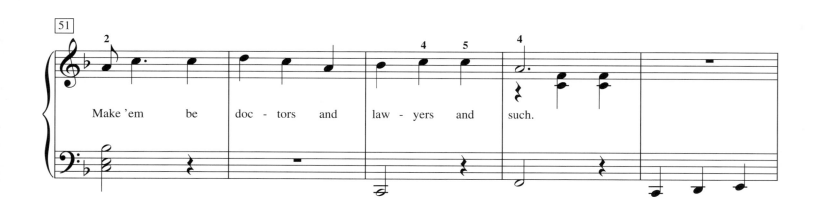

Make 'em be doc - tors and law - yers and such.

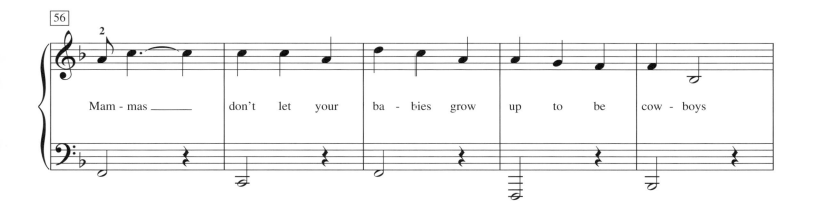

Mam - mas _____ don't let your ba - bies grow up to be cow - boys

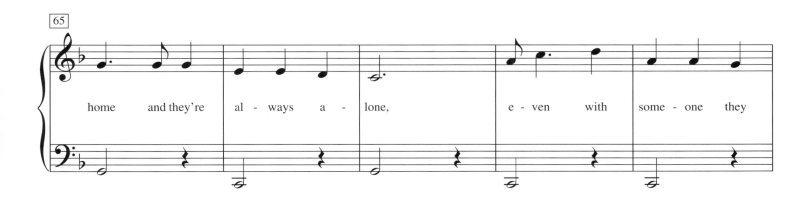

'cause they'll nev - er stay

home and they're al - ways a - lone, e - ven with some - one they

love. Mam - mas

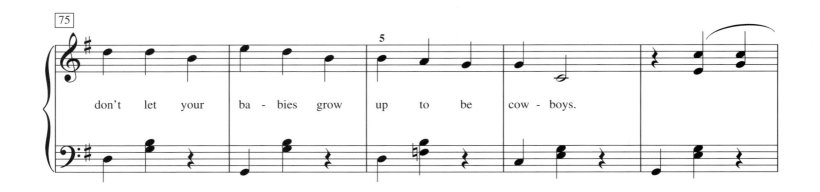

don't let your ba - bies grow up to be cow - boys.

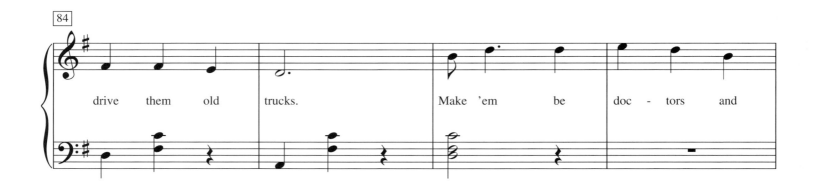

Don't let 'em pick gui - tars and

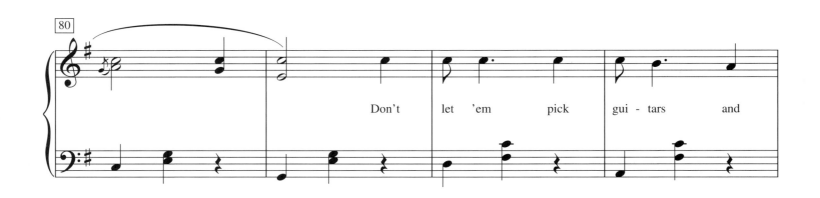

drive them old trucks. Make 'em be doc - tors and

law - yers and such. Mam - mas

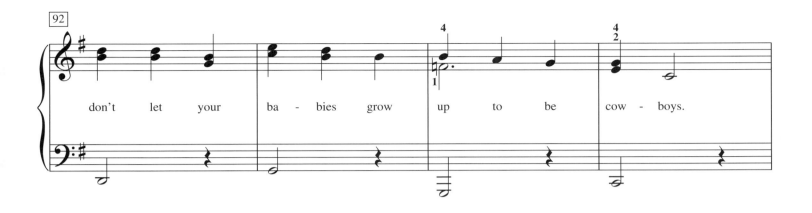

don't   let   your   ba – bies   grow   up   to   be   cow – boys.

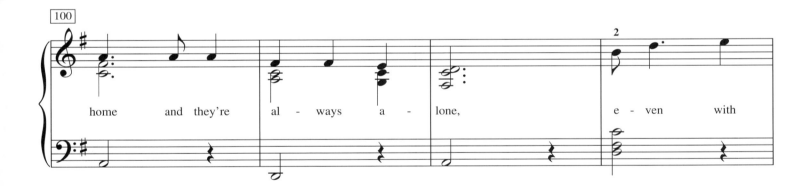

'cause they'll   nev – er   stay

home   and they're   al – ways   a – lone,   e – ven   with

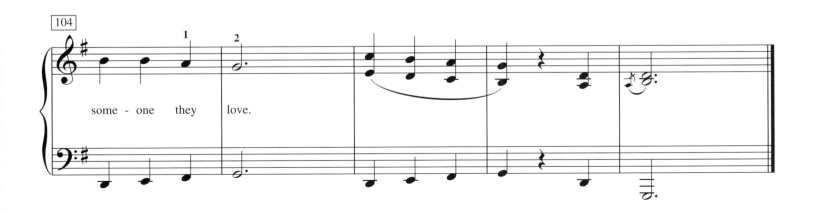

some – one   they   love.

Rocky Top

Words and Music by Boudleaux Bryant
and Felice Bryant
Arranged by Mona Rejino

Lively (♩ = 60)

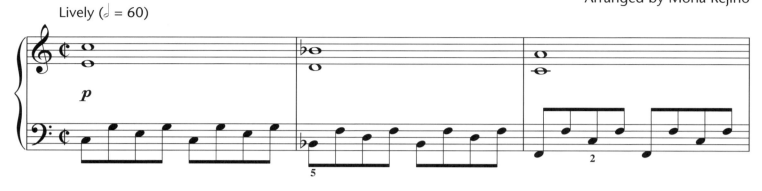

Wish that I was on ol' Rock - y Top,
Once two stran - gers climbed ol' Rock - y Top,

down in the Ten - nes - see hills. Ain't no smog - gy
look - in' for a moon - shine still. Stran - gers ain't come

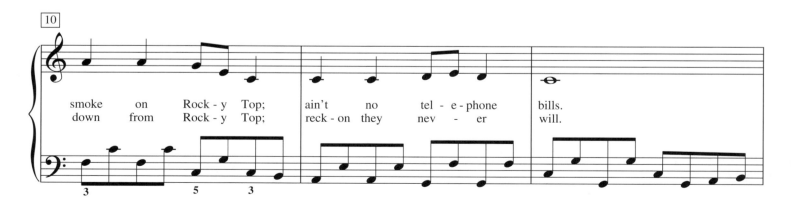

smoke on Rock - y Top; ain't no tel - e - phone bills.
down from Rock - y Top; reck - on they nev - er will.

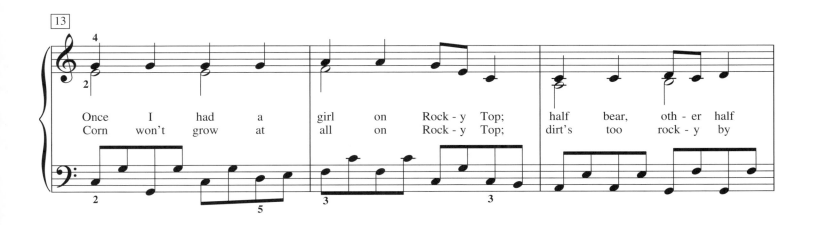

Once I had a girl on Rock-y Top; half bear, oth-er half
Corn won't grow at all on Rock-y Top; dirt's too rock-y by

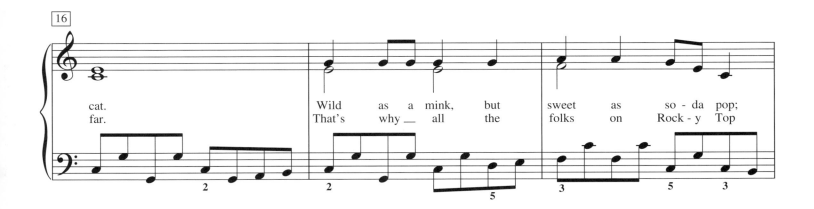

cat. Wild as a mink, but sweet as so-da pop;
far. That's why ___ all the folks on Rock-y Top

I still dream a-bout that. ⎰ Rock-y Top, you'll
get their corn from a jar. ⎱ *mf*

al - ways be home, sweet home to me. Good ol'

37

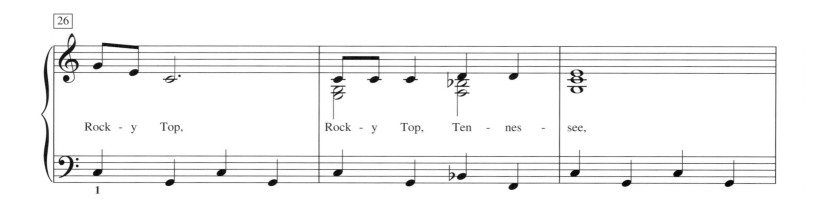

Rock - y Top,   Rock - y Top, Ten - nes - see,

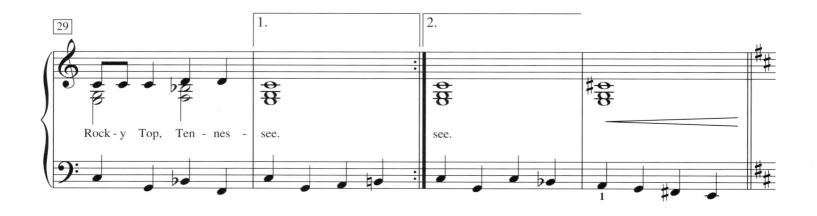

1.   2.

Rock - y Top, Ten - nes - see.   see.

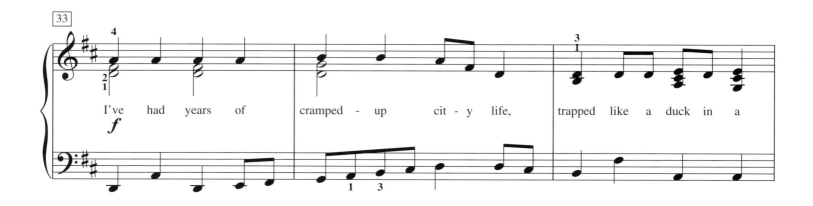

I've had years of cramped - up cit - y life, trapped like a duck in a

pen.   All I know is it's a pit - y life

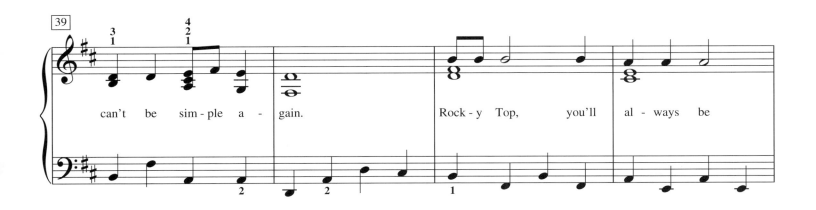

can't be sim - ple a - gain. Rock - y Top, you'll al - ways be

home, sweet home to me. Good ol' Rock - y Top,

Rock - y Top, Ten - nes - see, Rock - y Top, Ten - nes -
mf

see, Rock - y Top, Ten - nes - see.
f

POPULAR SONGS
HAL LEONARD STUDENT PIANO LIBRARY

The **Hal Leonard Student Piano Library** has great songs, and you will find all your favorites here: Disney classics, Broadway and movie favorites, and today's top hits. These graded collections are skillfully and imaginatively arranged for students and pianists at every level, from elementary solos with teacher accompaniments to sophisticated piano solos for the advancing pianist.

The Beatles
arr. Eugénie Rocherolle
Intermediate piano solos. Songs: *Can't Buy Me Love • Get Back • Here Comes the Sun • Martha My Dear • Michelle • Ob-La-Di, Ob-La-Da • Revolution • Yesterday.*
00296649 Correlates with HLSPL Level 5.........$10.99

Broadway Hits
arr. Carol Klose
Early-Intermediate/Intermediate piano solos. Songs: *Beauty and the Beast • Circle of Life • Do-Re-Mi • It's a Grand Night for Singing • The Music of the Night • Tomorrow • Where Is Love? • You'll Never Walk Alone.*
00296650 Correlates with HLSPL Levels 4/5 .....$7.99

Chart Hits
arr. Mona Rejino
8 pop favorites carefully arranged at an intermediate level. Songs: *Bad Day • Boston • Everything • February Song • Home • How to Save a Life • Put Your Records On • What Hurts the Most.*
00296710 Correlates with HLSPL Level 5 ....$7.99

Christmas Cheer
arr. Phillip Keveren
Early Intermediate level. For 1 Piano/4 Hands. Songs: *Caroling, Caroling • The Christmas Song • It Must Have Been the Mistletoe • It's Beginning to Look like Christmas • Rudolph the Red-Nosed Reindeer • You're All I Want for Christmas.*
00296616 Correlates with HLSPL Level 4...........$6.95

Christmas Time Is Here
arr. Eugénie Rocherolle
Intermediate level. For 1 piano/4 hands. Songs: *Christmas Time Is Here • Feliz Navidad • Here Comes Santa Claus (Right Down Santa Claus Lane) • I'll Be Home for Christmas • Little Saint Nick • White Christmas.*
00296614 Correlates with HLSPL Level 5...........$7.99

Classic Joplin Rags
arr. Fred Kern
Intermediate/Late Intermediate. Six quintessential Joplin rags arranged by Fred Kern: *Bethena (Concert Waltz) • The Entertainer • Maple Leaf Rag • Pineapple Rag • Pleasant Moments (Ragtime Waltz) • Swipesy (Cake Walk).*
00296743 Correlates with HLSPL Level 5 ....$6.95

Contemporary Movie Hits
arr. by Carol Klose, Jennifer Linn and Wendy Stevens
Six blockbuster movie favorites arranged for intermediate-level piano solo: *Bella's Lullaby • Breaking Free • Dawn • Georgiana • He's a Pirate • That's How You Know.*
00296780 Correlates with HLSPL Level 5..........$8.99

Contemporary Pop Hits
arr. Wendy Stevens
Seven top hits your late elementary students will love to learn! Includes: *All the Right Moves (OneRepublic) • Baby (Justin Bieber) • Breakout (Miley Cyrus) • Hey, Soul Sister (Train) • Love Story (Taylor Swift) • Lovebug (Jonas Brothers) • When I Look at You (Miley Cyrus).*
00296836 Correlates with HLSPL Level 3........$8.99

Current Hits
arr. Mona Rejino
Seven of today's hottest hits by artists such as Coldplay, Daughtry and Leona Lewis arranged as intermediate solos. Includes: *Apologize • Bleeding Love • Bubbly • Love Song • No One • Viva La Vida • What About Now.*
00296768 Correlates with HLSPL Level 5..........$8.99

Disney Favorites
arr. Phillip Keveren
Late-Elementary/Early-Intermediate piano solos. Songs: *Beauty and the Beast • Circle of Life • A Dream Is a Wish Your Heart Makes • I'm Late; Little April Shower • A Whole New World (Aladdin's Theme) • You Can Fly! • You'll Be in My Heart.*
00296647 Correlates with HLSPL Levels 3/4 .....$9.99

Disney Film Favorites
arr. Mona Rejino
Students of all ages will delight in Mona Rejino's intermediate arrangements of eight beloved Disney classics: *Cruella De Vil • Friend like Me • Go the Distance • God Help the Outcasts • Scales and Arpeggios • True Love's Kiss • When She Loved Me • You Are the Music in Me.*
00296809 Correlates with HLSPL Level 5 ....$10.99

Getting to Know You – Rodgers & Hammerstein Favorites
Illustrated music book. Elementary/Late Elementary piano solos with teacher accompaniments. Songs: *Bali H'ai • Dites-Moi (Tell Me Why) • The Farmer and the Cowman • Getting to Know You • Happy Talk • I Whistle a Happy Tune • I'm Gonna Wash That Man Right Outa My Hair • If I Loved You • Oh, What a Beautiful Mornin' • Oklahoma • Shall We Dance? • Some Enchanted Evening • The Surrey with the Fringe on Top.*
00296613 Correlates with HLSPL Level 3 ....$12.95

Glee
arr. Jennifer Linn
Jennifer Linn provides intermediate-level solo arrangments of seven favorites from *Glee*: *Don't Stop Believin' • Endless Love • Imagine • Jump • Lean on Me • Proud Mary • True Colors.*
00296834 Correlates with HLSPL Level 5 ....$10.99

Elton John
arr. Carol Klose
8 classic Elton John songs arranged as intermediate solos: *Can You Feel the Love Tonight • Candle in the Wind • Crocodile Rock • Goodbye Yellow Brick Road • Sorry Seems to Be the Hardest Word • Tiny Dancer • Written in the Stars • Your Song.*
00296721 Correlates with HLSPL Level 5 ....$7.95

Joplin Ragtime Duets
arr. Fred Kern
Features full-sounding, intermediate-level arrangements for one piano, four hands of: *Heliotrope Bouquet • Magnetic March • Peacherine Rag • The Ragtime Dance.*
00296771 Correlates with HLSPL Level 5 ....$7.99

Jerome Kern Classics
arr. Eugénie Rocherolle
Intermediate level. Students young and old will relish these sensitive stylings of enduring classics: *All the Things You Are • Bill • Can't Help Lovin' Dat Man • I've Told Ev'ry Little Star • The Last Time I Saw Paris • Make Believe • Ol' Man River • Smoke Gets in Your Eyes • The Way You Look Tonight • Who?*
00296577 Correlates with HLSPL Level 5 ....$12.99

Melody Times Two
Classic Counter-Melodies for Two Pianos, Four Hands
arr. Eugénie Rocherolle
This collection of classic counter-melody songs features four elegant and thoroughly entertaining arrangements for two pianos, four hands. Includes a definition and history of counter-melodies throughout musical periods; song histories; and composer biographies. The folio includes two complete scores for performance. Intermediate Level 4 Duos: *Baby, It's Cold Outside • Play a Simple Melody • Sam's Song • (I Wonder Why?) You're Just in Love.*
00296360 Intermediate Duets $12.95

Movie Favorites
arr. Fred Kern
Early-Intermediate/Intermediate piano solos. Songs: *Forrest Gump (Feather Theme) • Hakuna Matata • My Favorite Things • My Heart Will Go On • The Phantom of the Opera • Puttin' On the Ritz • Stand by Me.*
00296648 Correlates with HLSPL Levels 4/5 .....$6.99

Sing to the King
arr. Phillip Keveren
These expressive arrangements of popular contemporary Christian hits will inspire and delight intermediate-level pianists. Songs include: *By Our Love • Everlasting God • In Christ Alone • Revelation Song • Sing to the King • Your Name • and more.*
00296808 Correlates with HLSPL Level 5 ....$8.99

Sounds of Christmas (Volume 3)
arr. Rosemary Barrett Byers
Late Elementary/Early Intermediate level. For 1 piano/4 hands. Songs: *Blue Christmas • Christmas Is A-Comin' (May God Bless You) • I Saw Mommy Kissing Santa Claus • Merry Christmas, Darling • Shake Me I Rattle (Squeeze Me I Cry) • Silver Bells.*
00296615 Correlates with HLSPL Levels 3/4 .....$7.99

Today's Hits
arr. Mona Rejino
Intermediate-level piano solos. Songs: *Bless the Broken Road • Breakaway • Don't Know Why • Drops of Jupiter (Tell Me) • Home • Listen to Your Heart • She Will Be Loved • A Thousand Miles.*
00296646 Correlates with HLSPL Level 5...........$7.99

You Raise Me Up
arr. Deborah Brady
Contemporary Christian favorites. Elementary-level arrangements. Optional teacher accompaniments add harmonic richness. Songs: *All I Need • Forever • Open the Eyes of My Heart, Lord • We Bow Down • You Are So Good to Me • You Raise Me Up.*
00296576 Correlates with HLSPL Levels 2/3 .....$7.95

Visit our web site at **www.halleonard.com/hlspl.jsp** for all the newest titles in this series and other books in the Hal Leonard Student Piano Library.